The Bone-Orchard Conga

Performance Poems by Ray McNiece

Poetry Alive! Publications, Asheville, North Carolina

The Bone-Orchard Conga

© Copyright Third Edition 1997 Raymond McNiece

All rights reserved. No part of this book may be used or reproduced in any manner without written permission, except in the case of brief quotations embodied in critical articles or reviews.

Acknowledgment is gratefully made to the magazines and anthologies in which these poems were first published: **American Living,** "Once You Uncover," and "Snapshots of the Void." **Asheville Poetry Review,** "The Callings," "The Skin of Oroboros," and "The Annunciation." **Atelier,** "The Inevitable Movement of Love." **Black River Review,** "The Stretch of River Between Belpre and Marietta." **Blue Ox Review,** "Winter Solstice." **The Coffeehouse Anthology,** "Crazy Heart." **Naked City,** "On the Trolley Ride Home from Work." **Poetry on Stage,** "Turn It Off." **Red Brick Review,** "Grandfather's Breath." **Voices of Cleveland, Bicentennial Anthology,** "The Revenge of Cleveland."

The poems "A Coupla Stupid Animals" and "Disneyland" first appeared in different versions, in **DIS -- Voices from a Shelter (Burning Press © 1990).** A video version of "Boston Driving" was a winner of the **1994 San Francisco Poetry Film and Video Awards,** and was part of an installation at the **Decordova Museum in Massachusetts.** Excerpts from "Fly" appeared on the Boston MBTA poster series sponsored by **The National Writer's Union.**

Illustrations: Used by permission.
Cover : © Michael Shores.
Page 9 : © Angela Mark.
Page 31 : © Angela Mark.
Page 50 : © Michael Shores.
Page 74 : © Michael Shores.
Page 93 : © Michael Shores.
Back Cover Photo: © Eric Antoniou.

POETRY ALIVE! PUBLICATIONS

Library of Congress Catalog Card Number: 94-65383
ISBN# 1-883731-08-9

Many thanks to the many folks
who have helped me along the way
with a space to do this dance
and a place to rest my bones,
see you on the conga line.

THE BONE-ORCHARD CONGA

The Piper	7
Old Boyce	11
The Laughing Lady of Cleveland	13
Grandfather's Breath	14
Business as Usual	16
The Wash-Rag	18
On the Trolley Ride Home from Work	19
On My Back	21
Lunch Hour	23
The Bone-Orchard Conga	24
Boston Driving	26
The Revenge of Cleveland	29
The Real Deal	33
The End of the South End	36
Delirium Tremens	38
This Is How It Happens	39
I Learned to Get Even in the Can	41
Turn it Off!	42
A Coupla Stupid Animals	44
A Few Good Men	46
Click	49
The Callings	52
The Sustenance of Light	54
Winter Holy Water	56
Old Woman in a Slovenian Church in Cleveland	57
The Purgatory of Sister Margaret Merciless	58
From the Shining Eyes Staring Back from the Woods	60
Annunciation	62
Baptism	63
The Stretch of River Between Belpre and Marietta	66
Skinnydipping the Ganges	68
Waking at Evening	69
Winter Solstice	70
Dogwood Blossoms	71
After Talking Long into the Night	72
Coming From Fathoms Down Where Impulses Glow	73

Once You Uncover	76
Snapshots of the Void	77
The White Birds of Purgatory	78
Before the Downturn of the Bloodwheel	80
Young Woman Crossing a Field	81
Hide and Seek	82
Disneyland	83
Crazyheart	85
First Woman on the Moon	88
Night Song	89
The Skin of Oroboros	90
The Inevitable Movement of Love	92
Fly	95

The Piper

Were you the one I was tellin' about the Piper?
There ain't nothin' on this green and blue dustball,
nothin' that walks, crawls, leaps, limps, flies, falls,
swims or slimes across the bottom of the sea
that ain't but gotta pay the Piper - eventually.

Now you might think you're free and easy
and in the clear, that you stole away
with that last piece of pie when nobody was lookin',
that you slipped by when the Piper was sleepin'.
But that cat naps with one eye open

and hand on horn ready to squeeze those last few
sharp notes bring you flat to your knees
cryin', "Please, please, just a few more minutes.
I've got money." But the Piper don't need no
dough-ray-me make you fall-so-low. The Piper blows.

Sooner or later everyone gonna walk that bottom line.
Even them that got more money than God,
hidin' in their vaults, surrounded by bars of gold,
gonna hear that tune callin' their fading name.
Now how they gonna fly home wearin' all those chains?

You were the one I saw stop and loan that man
a fin when he was down so long, so low
it did not even cross his mind to get up and go,
holdin' the empty stem of his palm out
hopin' a green bird of paradise would feather his nest.

So you lost five and it cost you. It's only loot.
Maybe he found enough to buy a new pair of used boots
so he can pull himself up and take the next step
right in front of a subway in full-tilt, rush-hour commute.
Every busybody headin' up that same tunnel of light.

The buck don't stop here, there or anywhere
without clogging up the flow. Let it go.
The Piper plays the tune of skin and bones,
there, just below the surface, you hear the flow
telling you who, what, when, where -- how are you?

They say "You pays your money, you takes your chances."
Don't worry if you're prepared for the 'final expense.'
All the Piper plays is the only dance there is,
spinning you around once more to face the music
to balance you into...Can I have this dance?

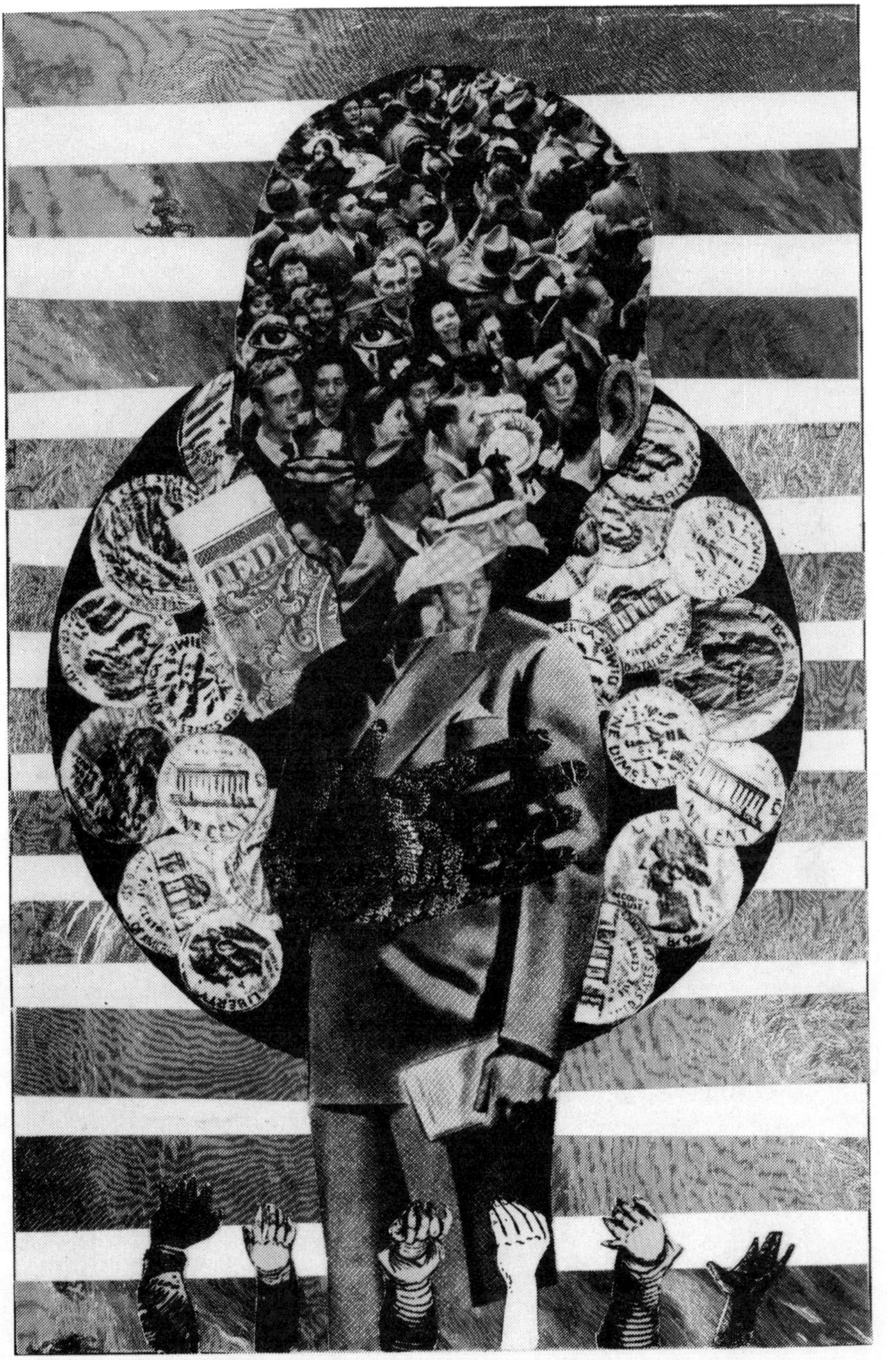

Old Boyce

Tired. Tired as steel
slugs. Piles of 'em,
size of quarters, rusting
out back behind
the Murray property,
former tank plant,
toy factory after that.

Tons of slugs, dumped
by some dinosaur machine
out back behind where
something too blue
percolates up
through gravel cinders
on hot days -
and it ain't sky.
and dead rainbows
belly-up in oilslicks.
Ain't no pot o' gold, Boyce.
Ain't no pot o' gold.

Old Boyce, who's squat
like something heavy
fell on him
long time ago,
wheezin' out of the same
dirty jokes in the same
bare-bulb, low-ceiling shop
year after year dipping
bumpers into troughs
of chemicals,
chromin' 'em,
chromin' 'em.

Boyce goin' bald
every hair in his nose
scorched out, the skin fused.
Boyce goin' blind,
drives his rustbucket car
with its shiny bumpers
past them piles of slugs
every goddamned day
til one day he stops it,

drags his baggy ass over,
punches both hands in
and pulls out fistfulls,
the burrs bitin'
into his grimy palms
til he bleeds,
til he drops
everything and stares

at the empty mirror
of his hands,
and tastes that
rusty mixture-
hack-ptu -- his life.

The Laughing Lady of Cleveland

Euclid Beach Park rickety rollercoaster screeches
over tinny pipe-organ drowning out ballbearing
factory ringing through immigrant Slav ears.
Tilt-a-wheel farts diesel while clearbulbs pop
an electric taste on tongue like pennies sucked.
Sticky cotton-candy hands clutch arcade prizes,
plastic soldiers, kewpies, orange marzipan peanuts,
while sweaty crowds crowd along in Taiwan elastic
polyesters plastered over fried-food clammy skin.

Do I remember her? How could I forget -- eight feet tall
and bigger in our fears, she guarded the "fun-house."
Grown-ups always stopped in front of her first
as she cranked back and forth on rusting steel spine,
hands on squat hips over potato dumpling legs.
Laughing Sal had gap-teeth, slug lips, flaring nostrils
and wore a loud, yellow dress with red polka dots.
Her garbled, vibrating hysterics would not let up
no matter where you were in the park, no matter
how many pillows you put over your head that night.

She was crazy mirror for Slovenian great-aunts,
Rose and Flo and Josie. By god, they needed to let go.
After the din of machines from seven to three,
after coming home to scrub linoleum and formica,
after resting their backs and soaking their feet,
they had to laugh. Behind them, bug-eyed, we stared.
Looking from them to her, we laughed and laughed, rickety
rollercoaster carrying us up clinka, clinka, clinka
almost as high as smokestacks in the sulphurous flats --
plummeting we screamed, throwing hands in air, sticky prizes
raining down on the heads of Rose and Flo and Josie.

Grandfather's Breath

"You work. You work, Buddy. You work."
Word of immigrant get-ahead grind I hear
huffing through me, Grandfather's breath
when he'd come in from Saturday's keep-busy chores,
fending up a calloused hand to stop
me from helping him, haggard cheeks puffing
out like work clothes hung between tenements,
doubled-over under thirty-five years a machine
repairman at the ballbearing factory,
ballbearings making everything run smoother --
especially torpedoes. He busted butt
for the war effort, for profiteers, for overtime pay
down-payment on a little box of his own,
himself a refugee of the European economy
washed ashore after the "war to end all wars,"
cheap labor for the winners.

I hear his youth plodding through the hayfields
above Srednevas, and the train that wheezed
and lumbered to the boat where he heave-hoed
consumptive sisters one, two, overboard.
I hear him scuffling along the factory-smoke choked
streets of Cleveland, coughing out chunks of broken
English -- how he grunted out a week's worth of grime
hurling ballincas down the pressed dirt court,
a sweaty wisp of grey hair wagging from his forehead,
"This is how the world turns. You work hard. You practice."
I hear his claim as we climbed the steps of the Stadium,
higher, into the cheap seats, slapping the flat of this hand
against a girder, "I built this, Buddy."

But mostly I hear how he'd catch
what was left of his breath after Saturday's keep-busy chores,
pouring out that one, long, tall, cold beer
that Grandma allowed him, and holding it aloft,
the bubbles golden as the hayfields above Srednevas.
He'd savor it down before taking up the last task
of his day off, cleaning the cage,
letting Snowball, canary like the ones once used
to test coal-mines for poison air, flap clumsily free
around the living room, crapping on
the plastic covered davenport and easychairs
they only sat in twice a year.

And I'm still breathing, Grandpa, the day you took me
down the basement to the cool floor to find out
what was wrong. "C'mon, Snowball, fly. C'mon, fly."
The bird splayed out on the same linoleum
where they found you, next to your iron lung,
where Grandma mopped for weeks afterwards,
pointing with arthritic fingers, "See, there,
there's where he fell and bumped his head.
See the specks of blood." She can't work out.
One fine morning when my work is done,
I'm gonna fly away home.
"C'mon Snowball, fly. Fly."

Business As Usual

What are you gonna do,
sit around inside all day
watchin' the news flash on
and off while the sun pours in
through a big hole in the ozone?
What are you gonna do, sit around
thinkin' about it? You thinkin' about it
you start worryin', you start worryin'
you get stressed out, you get stressed out
you get all balled up inside,
you know what I mean,
you get all balled up!
You get depressed, deeepressed.
The bottom falls out. The bottom falls out,
all hell breaks loose.

What are you gonna do,
miss a day of work? Pretty soon
you miss another day.
You don't think the boss notices,
you don't think the boss notices?
What if everybody missed a day of work?
Who would cut out the coupons?

What are you gonna do,
sit around on your butt all day?
You sit around on your butt
you know what you get?
A fat butt, that's what.
You fall behind, you fall in arrears,
you gotta work twice as hard
to make it up. You're better off
maintainin' if you wanna keep
your assets covered.
You just gotta relax
and stay busy, that's all.
Relax and stay busy.

You gotta keep the ball rollin',
you gotta keep the ball rollin',
like one of those turd bugs
I saw on that nature show on TV.
They roll that turd ball
around the desert all day long.
They roll it up the hill,
it rolls back down.
They roll it up the hill,
it rolls back down.
It rolls away from them
they don't know what the hell to do.
You're not doin' somethin'
you're sittin' around worryin' about it,
etcetera, etcetera.

You wanna be like the grasshopper?
The grasshopper you read about in school.
You didn't read about it
by 8:30 sharp Wednesday morning
Sister Margaret Merciless
with her starched, creased face
crack you across the butt with a ruler,
"I'll give you something, I'll
give you something to cry about!"

You wanna be like the lazy grasshopper,
legs crossed, pickin' your teeth,
playin' your fiddle all summer.
The winter comes, you know what happens?
You freeze your butt off, that's what.
You're better off bein' like an ant,
an ant knows what to do,
it knows exactly what to do.
It goes from point A to point B,
from point A to point B. It's simple.
It stays in line, You gotta be
like an ant, like an ant!
Please leave a message after the beep!

The Wash Rag

On this bus grinding along coughing
exhaust on the already sooty snow,
one impulse limps through every body -- home.
The economy and emotion peaked at Christmas
like red and green lights in the trees.
Now all that's left is putting in time
and sitting tight for warmer weather.

The middle-aged women crushed in a row
avoid looking at each other, avoid
any complicity in this drudgery.
One of them, head bundled in multicolored
polyester, nods asleep. Another, her white
service clothes stained with orange blotches,
stares across with bitter coffee eyes.
Next to her, there's a woman whose face
is creased and cracked with gutters
that would carry tears if sorrow
were allowed on public transportation.

She's becoming a load of laundry she drags
up the stairs every evening after work.
At the kitchen sink, in dishwater that steams
the window grey, she warms hands that feel
like they were broken and never set right.
When she has had enough, she wrings out
the wash rag, hangs it over the spigot,
and looks at nothing in front of her.

On the Trolley Ride Home from Work

Man, when do we get a rest?
Where we manage the strength
to get up at the end of work
and shove onto the trolley
till it lurches and stutters out
of the tunnel away from the city,
stands as one of the drastic
measures of weekend to weekend.

I squeeze on, shift both aching feet,
and adjust my commuter face.
But something unavoidable happens
up on the far side of the car.
The crowd bends to a semicircle
around a man sitting on the edge.
He's jerking his fists up and down,
then pointing and wagging his finger,
scolding what remains unseen to us.

All of a sudden, he freezes,
glances this way and that,
jams his thick glasses back beneath
the dark furrow of his eyebrow,
and re-engages his thrashings.
The most mortal laugh I've ever
laughed jumps out of my face.
I must be working too much.

But how he generates the energy
to shake the cage of his body
must be one of the unexplainable
tantrums of the universe manifested,
order struggling to escape as chaos.
Or call him a textbook case,
how it's ingrained in his genes,
how it's a question of him being committed
to the asylum of his mind for life.
That still leaves him a man straining
to be free -- my brother in this city.

The woman next to him tilts away.
On the other side, she glares off.
She's mad and just wants to get home
with her groceries in one piece.
The rest of us stay at a distance
and hang from the ceiling like nerves:
taut or numb or kinked or drugged.
He keeps banging on some invisible
threshold as we stand at the metal doors
waiting to be released into the dark
walk that leads back to our own lives.

On My Back

Ever feel how damned hard it is
to find a mattress of just
the right consistency?
They're always either slab stiff,
or soft as a skeleton
preserving bog.

I curse Australopithicus for ever
having the nerve
to walk upright.
And as for this hairless biped's ambition,
reaching for the highest fruit
and not merely longing
for it to fall
in its own sweet time,
why in the hell
didn't they sit still
in bewildered naivte
on a mossy bank
and wait?

Now we break our backs
to scratch out the cash
to buy a stretch
to throw down our bones
at the end of our days.
Oh, sure, the pain is a gift,
a character builder,
a contrast to heaven even,
but no relieved angel could climb
to some cloud comfort
up this rickety ladder
without hearing about it.

If archeologists ever dig up this spine,
they'll read the habits
of the work ethic in each vertebrae,
speculating on my poor posture.
When they bend it,
they'll still be able to hear
this cranky pain in the neck
in the ass expressed
so fluently.

Lunch Hour
   for Steve Sundberg

After eating our junk-food in the Public Garden,
we lean back into the usual big small-talk,
asking each other why man constantly asks
questions he can never possibly answer
like life after death, and, if so, do we get a raise?

We've been painting the same wall the same
color for the last 2,000 years or so -- off-white.
It's necessary to think we're getting somewhere
like the businessmen who hurry by playing beat the clock.
The one with the most money at the end wins.

We say nothing we do or say is either crucial or trivial
to the pigeons that fall around us for a handout
and take up their hubbub of hungry bobbing.
We only have ten minutes left on our break
before we have to go back to earning our daily bread.

You eat a peach down to the pit that's too hard
to crack open to see the tree it could burst into.
You toss it into the duck pond, and we watch
as it sinks to the bottom of these kinds of riddles.
Then we go back to work where we won't think for hours.

The Bone-Orchard Conga

I shoulder on the crowded bus, stuff myself in a seat
and scrounge a sheet of stale news off the floor
to keep me busy until my stop.
When I glance up, it happens again --
seems like I've met each one of them before.

I let it pass and go back to the cartoons.
When I look up again, jostled by a stretch
of spine-jarring potholes, all their tired faces
begin to jiggle and jiggle and slide
off, revealing the intimate

anonymity of those sockets
and that smile. A smile parts my flesh,
curling my lips -- we've never lived,
we never die. We mate our skeletons,
hip bone connected to hip bone.

Death, my roommate, waits at home.
I sit down to eat dinner across from him.
He grinds a pinch of salt in my meal
that gives it an immediate taste,
then mimics my feeble chewing.

Death, you don't look so hot.
You ought to do something about those maggots.
You work too much -- which he does, leading
the marathon dancers who hold up
their corpses-to-be under chandelier stars.

We do the bone-orchard conga,
wobbling like babies. We do the dust
to dust shuffle, and the way-of-all-flesh
two-step, dipping a heartbreak tango
down into our rootcellar flops.

He tousles my hair before I fall
to sleep, before he leaves for the graveyard
shift, lunchbox full of the dust of poems.
Take it easy, I tell him. "Well, Buddy," he smiles,
glowing, "I'll see you tomorrow."

Boston Driving

He gave me, that large Boston driver,
what could be taken in no uncertain terms
as a universal sign of displeasure over the seven seas
and to these four corners -- he gave me the finger.

Well, what do you want? It was Mass. Ave.,
after all, and sure, I was taking some liberties
with the speed limit and the lane, but no matter what
he tells you, I did not cut him off -- not much.

Poking in off a cross-street, he should have known
better -- that captain of what looked like a trawler --
he should have known better than to challenge
the current of rush-hour, but damn the light

he chugged on through a fusillade of horns, that is,
almost through until me, and there we met,
skidding to a stop as if we were having
an argument that had to inevitably
intersect there, in a crescendo of adrenaline
and a conflagration of our mutual frustrations.

And in the suspended animation after the close call,
his gratitude for my bringing him
to the experience, for clearing his arteries
in a rush of his past flying before him,
expressed itself so simply in the slow raising
of his backhand, and the lone finger unfolding.

Maybe I was just too tired, but my first impulse
to jeer at it gave way. Something else opened.
I enjoyed it; I did what it came to me to do.
I said, in a manner of speaking, "Yeah,
you too," and realized, this is how the city talks.

I imagine us meeting again, duelling profanities,
gesticulating at each other, each
flaring with a more elaborate twist on the theme:
him working it up as if he were playing
"Flight of the Bumblebees" on a broken
accordion, and me -- arms folded, head cocked --
awaiting his finale so I can jack-knife up
like a deranged basketball referee
attempting to signal a personal foul
over the heads of the entire Celtics' lineup --
And we keep this mime of expletives going
until one of us busts a gut or floors the other.

Yep, I'm learning the intimate dialects
of this city. With one gesture I have become
a part of his day, of his life; one of the family,
a hand sticking up into his memory,
into the accumulated chronicle
of his day to day so on and so on
struggles, aggravations, and lack of laughter.
Hell, maybe I did burn his ulcer deeper.

But his hand -- how it opens thickly and beckons,
the stiff fingers he cracked and crooked to rub
his eyes after straining over the morning paper;
that he picked his profusely-haired nose with,
that got slammed in the door yesterday,
that were almost sheared off at work last year,
that tickled the nipples of his heavy wife's
heavy breasts -- she who wears an impervious
resolve, who keeps a low balance to weather
his hollerings, who has her own hands and work
to do, and she puts up with his bitching too.

He might focus, some drunk night, on each of those
fingers and see how they are all part of the hard
fisting and stretching that he stares at, testing
its potential for damage -- its clumsy grace.
A hand that he looks at come morning as if it
sprouted overnight, wondering what trouble
it's been into or what good it's done, but
never aware of the simple message it had given to me.

The Revenge of Cleveland
a menu against nouvelle cuisine

At a restaurant a la arboretum in a trendy alley
back of Harvard Square, I sit down
to a platter of minimalist philosophy
and wait for more.
When none comes I realize this is
the entree, and it hits me -- this will cost!
Three slivers of salmon looking, for the life of them,
like playdough cutouts, a spot
of goose liver pate nudged
under a scrap of spinach grown in a petri dish,
an upscale garnish of designer legumes,
and, existentially enough, a single olive
sans pimento. The whole plate could be
a display of new-wave jewelry.

Enough of this "less is more."
More is more, and I want some!
Let's start with dumpling soup, the aroma
buoyed by globules of chicken fat --
the hundred suns that never shine on gray Cleveland --
then the dumplings themselves, behemoths
of cholesterolled ambrosia. Bring on the pirogues,
and put a tub of cheez-whiz
made from artificial imitation processed cheesefood
at one elbow, and on the other side, a mound
of sauerkraut steaming like the Cuyahoga
stirred by a scow on a Spring morning.
Eggnoodles too, rolled and cut and ladled
by my heavy, old country great-aunts.
And oh, the loaves of seed-chocked rye
and pumpernickel smeared with lard.
Give me a bellyful of kielbasi inspired indigestion
anyday -- the revenge of Cleveland --
a pile that makes you spout,
"Lay on, MacDuffski, and let no mouth cry,
'Hold, enough.'"

To top it off, a roll of peticza,
and a quivering dollop of pink-Jell-O salad
straight from a Stuckey's off the western pike,
all frothed with non-dairy whip.

So, none of this lightweight stuff
that lets you off to play squash or the stocks.
None of this nuance and dabble on the palate.
I want a heap of carbohydrates so I can't move
the rest of the afternoon, chowed down in a bar
with the Brown's game blaring.
A meal as heavy and profound as an Immigrant Cathedral,
as bland and fulfilling as a busload of Slovenians
coming home from Polka Varieties,
dreaming of Sunday dinner.

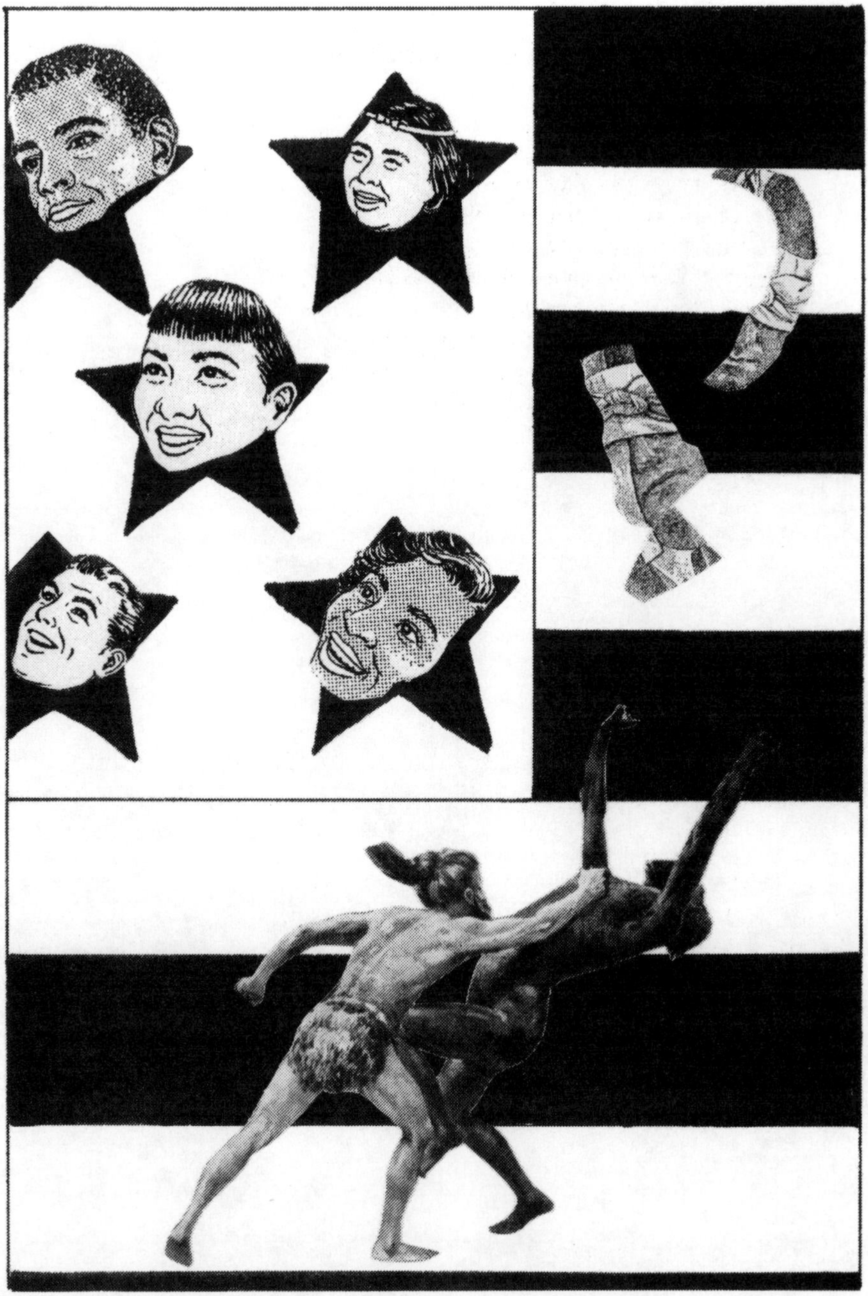

The Real Deal

As they walk past us, one lady says to the other
"The poor will always be with us," I say, Lady,
how come nobody ever says nothing about the rich
always bein' with us? Those skyscrapers look familiar?
High priests in three-piece suits set the clocks,
sign the checks, and we grind our bones into dust --
cuttin' down trees, rollin' blocks into place,
cities risin', deserts spreadin' for four thousand years
of civilization. Babylon got its name from Babylon.

Why do we take it? Why don't we just take off
our wristwatches? We want that pie in the sky.
That's the carrot on the stick, gold medal on high,
brass ring on the merry-go-round, go directly
to jail, do not pass go, do not collect two-hundred dollars.
We're busy tryin' to stay ahead of the game,
only they keep changin' the rules on us.
You start off easy enough, heading for what you want.
What you think you want. You seen it on TeeVee.
You want the cheese -- like everybody else.
You can smell it. You can see yourself tasting it,
squeezin' your beady little eyes -- mmm.

So you start off runnin', bumpin' offa walls,
bumpin' offa the same wall for years
til your head dulls. You can't go through it.
There ain't no shortcut. So you go around.
And around. And before too long you forget
where you came from and you just sit
right down wherever you are and watch TeeVee
and wait for it to come to you like the lottery.

Only, it never does. After a while you give up
on the cheese and take what they give you --
those big bricks of government cheese
in cardboard boxes. An it ain't even Velveeta, man.
Or you take what you can get and find yourself
sitting in a big cage with all the other rats,
and they're as angry and as hungry as you are.
And that man on TeeVee, he's smilin' at you.
He's asking you, "What are you doing up so late?"
"You should be comfortably asleep by now
on a water flotation device."

But we hold on to those measly little TeeVee dreams
cause we're better off than those sorry-ass poor
over in Africa with their bloated stomachs,
their shrivelled brains, and withered hands. Right.
Take a look around. Does this look like a **Dynasty**
episode? Does this look like the land of cheese?
You know there's alotta data on TeeVee -- a whole
lotta data. But you can tell what's goin' on
not by what they show you, but by what
they don't show you. That's the real deal.
You gotta learn to read, to read between the lines.

I seen them crack rats on the tube. They give them
a little taste of crack and put them in a cage
with a pile of food at one end and a vial of crack
at the other and an electrified grill between.
That rat runs across that grill to get a hit
over and over and over till his feet fry off.
Now they're usin' that rat to show how bad
crack is cause the rat wants it so bad.
But maybe they're askin' that rat the wrong question.
Maybe what the rat is sayin is "I want out of this cage!"
cause one dead end is as good as the next.

Last night when I turned off the news,
I saw my own face starin' back at me
from the blank screen. I saw my own face
lookin' back from this here situation
and I am not comfortably asleep
on a water flotation device.

The End of the South End

Monday morning busies with progress
at the intersection of Mass. Ave. and Columbus,
the very end of the South End of Boston.
Five-story redbrick rowhouses are being gutted,
fitted with fixtures shiny as new money,
and wrought-iron bar burglar-proofed.
From sidewalk cracks, frozen explosions of ragweed
snag the weathered skin of last week's stock pages
as a three-legged dog cringes and an old dude
tap-tap-taps along rush hour's kamikazes.
Our Lady of the shopping bags pushes a buggy
full of empties towards redemption as MC Jam
boom-boom-boom! boxes along, scouring flying rats
from curbs and rapping backs of business heads
who ride behind the wave of heavy equipment
blitzkrieging in from real-estate towers downtown.
A man sticks his head out a window and screams --
It's either the end of the world or another day.

Weekend party nights, the sun burned down rusty
as an oil drum fire warming a vacant lot.
Bloated and already drunk, the moon bellied up
and pissed splinters of glass all over the alley.
Inside the 501 Jazz Club a standing room only crowd
jammed with a last stand of ghosts from the heydays.
Grim, unfairytale children claimed the last walls
with florescent hieroglyphs while young Turks
in Sparrow Park toked, joked, told lies and tried
to get laid, pipes glowing like lightning bugs.
On the corner a hooker turned on her four way smile
hot as a stoplight for the husbands of the suburbs
in front of the boarded-up Zion Fire Baptized Church
soon to be condo, down the block from a florist front
where, before the State lottery, numbers walked in
and luck strolled out crisp as a Franklin -- condo now,
like Arizona's Beauty shop, best fence in town,
next to the Paris Tonsure Mart where stories started
down home go on and on all afternoon -- condoed.

Old men setting on the steps of those abandonments
stay on a first name basis with their shadows,
emptying pints of Night Train to get out of town,
bare-bulb street light glaring from the ceiling sky
because nobody is high enough to swat it off.
Instead, this Monday morning, they rise wincing.
The sun, a dirty yellow truck, grinds up through
exhausted air as their dreams steam from manholes.
The future, she clicks down the street in a skirtsuit
and has to stop herself from looking over her shoulder.
She smiles, clutching contracts, the nervous smile
of prosperity, just around the corner, at the intersection
of Mass. Ave. and Columbus, the end of the South End.

Delirium Tremens

Sprawled on the sidewalk,
shivering in the thaw
after a long drunk,
nodding in and out,
the sun smacking his head,
He winces. His eyes untwist,
his face widens then screws
closed. He concentrates
on the dribble and hang
of his spit. He tries hard
but he can barely recall
one place, one face blurs
into another. He hasn't
slept to dream in too long
and the scenes have over-
lapped, and the passersby,
all his friends come
walking towards him, some
kick him by mistake, he
wakes and wakes to each kick.

This Is How It Happens

This is how it happens. Men wake up downsized.
They walk up to find the chainlink gate of the plant
padlocked. No call. They lose their pensions,
their place on line, their place in the unemployment line.
They lose their ability to look each other in the eyes
without quickly looking away. These men get together
to get drunk til they crush empty cans into their foreheads.

This is how it happens. Two men are walking closely,
laughing, maybe even the backs of their hands
brushing together, or their shoulders touching.
They come upon a group of men standing in a circle
in the back of the park around a pile
of crushed, empty beer cans. One of the two
smiles a greeting and hurries the other past
and just as they are almost out of earshot
they will hear it shouted again, a second time,
louder, so there can be no doubt what will happen next.

Here is how it happens. A young man hurries home
along a deserted street focused only on getting through
another day. He hears somebody echoing his footfalls
across the street. He looks up. A misstep. A mistake.
What are you lookin' at, punk? A crack.
A dark smudge and chalk outline on the sidewalk
the next day, washed away in a week.
And there is nowhere now it is not
the wrong place at the wrong time.

Here is how it happens. One man finds himself
down and out and wondering where it went wrong
not just for him, but for millions like him.
He rests at a vacant bus stop skimming headlines
of the latest reported brutalities
before turning to the sports' page,
before going back to collecting cans.

He hears a sound like shovels digging --
the scuffling of many feet. A group of men
approach carrying something between them.
He can't tell what it is until they are closer,
until they are almost right here.

I Learned to Get Even in the Can

Hey! What are you lookin at?
Look at this. Blood. My blood.
Two punks jumped me tonight.
I just got outa the slammer
3 days ago and 2 guys jump me.
I grabbed the kid's knife.

You should see them. Dead meat.
Those two-bit, half-assed punks
better be lookin over their shoulders
forever. I'll bide my time.
I'll study their movements.
I learned to get even in the can.

I don't wanna live at that level.
But I get even. I'll even double-back
into jail if that's what it takes.
I got out on good behavior for A&B,
found out who ratted me out, pulled
a B&E and waited for the cops.

When I got back in I just waited.
Told the guy it all blowed over.
Told him I believed he was framed.
Even gave him a big fatty
to show no hard feelings and all...
then did a hi-lo job on him.
He couldn't wank off for weeks.

I'm telling you, you can't cage me,
stick it to me on a daily basis
then let me out into this vicious
situation and expect me to be
rehabbed -- most of these cruds
ain't even been habilitated.
Next time I ain't gonna kill somebody,
I'm gonna kill every body.

Turn It Off

Cabs blaring for their fares to come down already,
car alarms hysterically yelping about property,
gape-jawed garbage trucks beep-beep-beeping ass-backwards
down alleys, heavy-metal insects scouring the sky escaping,
tonight the city is a pot of noise boiling over
over a greasy orange coil on the back burner,
while cockroaches type out fine-print apocalyptic editorials
on a carpet of dead news, and the sirens **we-you, we-you, We-You,
WE-YOU, We-You, we-you, we-you** never sleep.

And it's too god-damn hot to shut out the canned laughter
pummelling through the blue room across the alley,
or the car-chase screech shoot-em-ups accompanied
by muzak suspense and deodorant commercials,
or the ambulance on screen closing in, cut to close up --
a mother moaning her son's name into the rescue camera.
We want these horrific moments instant replayed,
that's why we got one-hundred and fifty channels of cable,
that's why the man deep in his black hole shouts,
"Turnnn it offf!" But the sirens **we-you, we-you, We-You,
WE-YOU, We-You, we-you, we-you** never sleep --

the same scream coming from the broken
body of the drunken wreck, from the gasping fish-face
of the heart-attack, from the still hungry ulcer
on the overdose's arm, from the gangreened mouth
of the bag-lady's boot, from the contorted, cried out face
of a baby blossomed with bruises, from the hole, hole, hole
poked through some punk looking the wrong way,
from 37 spluttering lips of a woman stabbed inside out **we-you,
we-you, We-You, WE-YOU, We-You, we-you, we-you**
all climbing to the top of the nightly news
to tell to no avail the war happening right here,
the sirens having come home to roost, hungry --

drilling memory like the four-faced megaphone
atop Immaculate Conception next to concrete cross,
testing its warning once a month, a cold war whine
cranking up to a science-fiction movie wail,
WeeeeeeeeHeeeeeeeeeYouuuuuuuu
mushroom clouds crowding out imagination
for five-minute drill, file into fallout shelter gym,
backs against walls too flimsy too withstand
shockwaves we watched stuttering out
on garbled Civil Defence training films.
It became routine as penance prayers
for sins we had to make up -- except at home
where I stockpiled canned goods in the basement
in the quiet under the washtubs
in case a real emergency obliterated the screen,
melting family poses into negatives, into lumps.

Tonight, I'm trying to return to the circle
of silence, the pond at the edge of the woods
of childhood, where bright sunfish churned
and fanned above spawning beds and hovered farther out
when startled **we-you, we-you, We-You, We-You, WE-YOU,
We-You, We-You, we-you, we-you** peels naked and bloody
down the middle of the street, and the man deep in his black
hole starts again, and it's too "TURN IT OFF!" goddamn hot
"TURN IT OFF!" to shut it all "TURN IT OFF!" out.

Coupla Stupid Animals

I come home, right. Home.
First thing they wanna to know,
"How many gooks you kill?"
How the hell do I know.
I was shootin' like crazy.

I do remember one guy
right at the beginning.
We surprised each other
and just stood there starin'--
coupla stupid animals.
He was N.V.A., kinda scrawny.

Musta been a new guy too,
'cause anybody been out longer
knows better.
We stood there starin' for three
maybe four seconds tops
and I drills him.

I was goin' through his pockets --
we was supposed to --
and I found a picture of his girl
and a little book. Plans,
I figured. I give it
to the translator.
He threw it away,
right in front of me.
"Poetry," he sez.
"They all write the crap."

Here I am in Viet Nam,
shorts rottin' off my butt,
cut and bit-up, scared shitless,
and this kid, and I mean,
he weren't more than a kid --
livin' on a handfulla rice a day --
is writing poetry?

How many did I kill?
Just the one
was enuf for me.

A Few Good Men

I'm not the problem.
Certain administrators at the V.A.
would like me to think
I'm the problem. Viet Nam
wasn't my problem. It became
my problem. Post Traumatic Stress
DISorder became my problem. Do you
have a problem with me being here
at this wall? Would you like one?
Hey, peace man. Peace.

If you raise your voice
down certain corridors in **WARshington**,
DeeCeased - there will be trouble.
You are to protest only in the
designated areas. The **PentaGOON**
is off-limits. The President's Ear
is verboten. He can't hear
because of the helicopter blades beating the air
because of the helicopter blades,
he can't hear!

I've been warned several times I am not allowed
to wail at this wall. I am not permitted
to raise my voice for my fallen comrades
in the Marine **CORPSE**. I am not permitted,
and that's my name there -
a computer error. A bureaucratic
oversight. A name, rank and serial number snafu.
Now you could deem me to be a problem.
You could even deem me to be
Missing in Action on the front lines
of the United States of **Annhilation**.
But I assure you I am not dead.
My syndrome is not buried.
I am not a ghost, sir.

Questions? I have a few
thousand questions. Why are concerned citizens
confronting me about their tax-dollars.
Is it my problem there are 20,000 vets
walking the streets somewhere between Nam and home,
and there are seven empty floors
two blocks from here. But there's not enough money
to send us over there. But there is
enough money to send us "over there."
Because it's more cost effective to house us
in Arlington National Cemetary.
This is the land of the bottom line after all.

I have my rights. I have the right
to speak out openly
and get a forty-day walking pass to Danang
where I have the right to kill
or be killed - I have that right.
I have the right to wait for a bed
in a treatment center for ten months
for a syndrome I feel every day even
unto my dreams. I have the right
to be wet sheet wrapped, electro-shocked and hosed
three times a day to be made a functioning member
of my **SUICIDITY** again.
Do you know how many bombs fell into me?
Ba-ba-ba-ba-Boom!   1/2 million Vietnamese,
Ba-ba-ba-ba-Boom!   1 million Cambodians,
Ba-ba-ba-ba-Boom!   60 thousand Americans,
Ba-ba-ba-ba-Boom!   300 thousand Iraqis and counting.
Just a little incontinent ordinance, Sir.
Just a little collateral damage, Sir.
War is a messy business afterall, Sir.
I was just doing my job, Sir.
It became necessary to destroy the world
in order to save it, Sir.

Questions? I have a few
questions. How many people
will be sacrificed for another person's
vertical aspirations and prosperity?
A few good men? A few
thousand? A few million? Hey,
peace, man. Peace.

Click

for R.R.
"Check, check. The bombing begins in five minutes. Heh, heh."

"Weh-weh-weh-welllll," the apple-cheeked, make-up caked puppet waves from ground-zero flats, surrounded by purple majesties of slag. Enthroned on a springy, bare-ribbed horse-hair easy-chair, he nods, tuned into Death Valley Days rerunning vista-vision on a blank screen.
His bobbing, brilliantine pompadour still fills with Hollywood puffs of grandeur as his marquee smile fizzles down orange.

But he's got a Bowl o'Speed at one elbow he pops while he clicks remotely, vaporizing instant gratification and zapping up a new improved jolt of youth forever for a limited time offer only $19.99...
click -- a smile-face Morning-in-America bulletted forehead blood drip
click -- televangelic tongue of profitcy reading the end-times report
click -- the last dollar of Eden crumbling in a hungry hand
click -- game show contestants chanting, "we want it all, we want it now!"
click -- bloat-bellied children staring at an aerobic instructor's routines
click -- genuine zirconian power-tie clips
click -- Gilligan's Island, everybody is stuck on Gilligan's Island
click -- Big Time Wrestling Cockroaches smashing a city to rubble
click -- highlights of missiles homing in on targets
click -- click -- click --how easy the spark flies from the finger
click -- a cartoon mushroom KERBLOOMY!
click -- back to Death Valley Days, he sees himself watching and
click -- click -- click -- but the picture stays static.

Outside the chain-link, barb-wired private property,
Coyote turns and peers back from the sunset, hacks out a plastic doll and lets loose a howl through the red, white and blue corroding sky, blowing away the black smoke spelling out THE END.
His call pierces as clear as a single drop of rain on a cactus spike, as fierce as a desert blossom opening by dawn's early light.

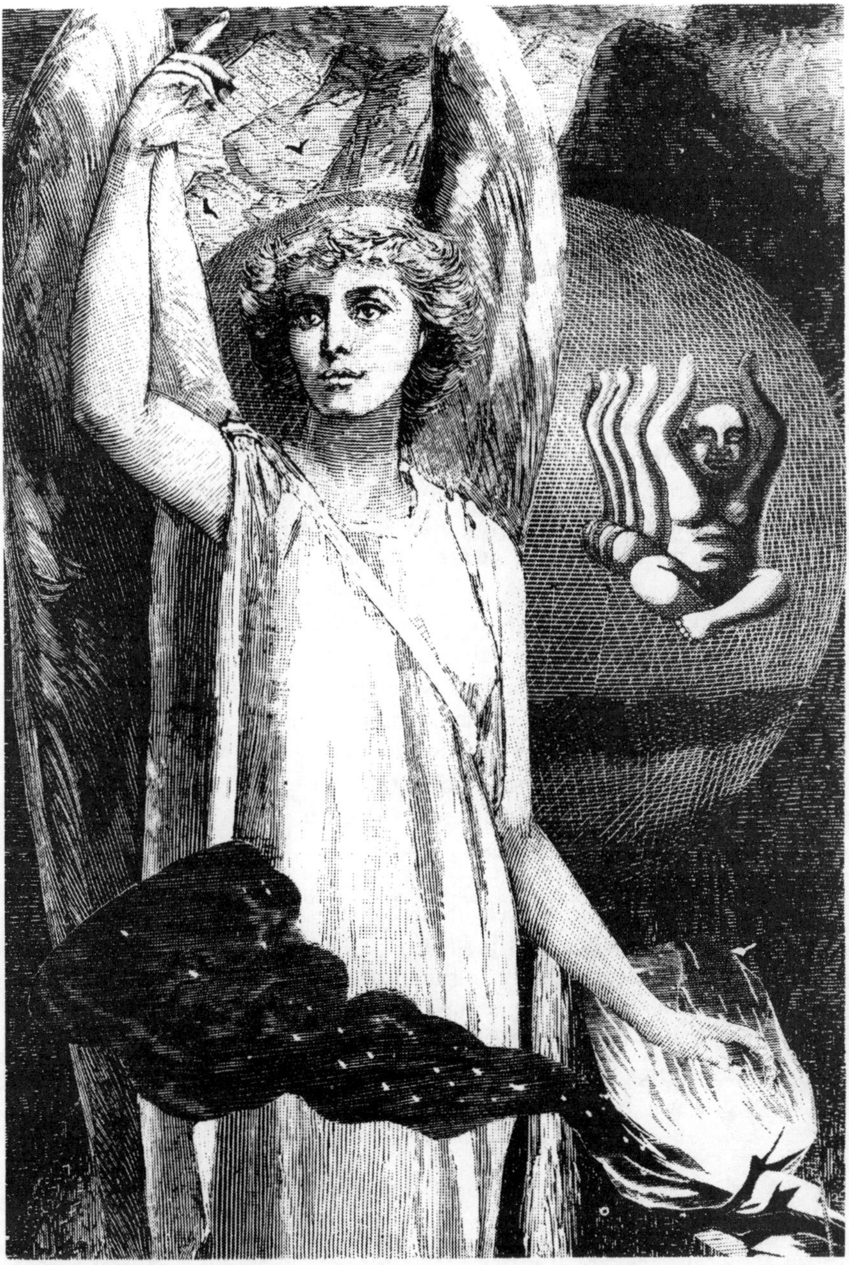

The Callings

*Have you heard? Brothers and sisters,
you may have been way down in the hole,
you may have been on top of the world
you may just have been walking dully along.
Have you heard the call?*

Sundays came a light that baptized
the warped, whitewashed boards of the Layman Church.
Inside it swirled along the brown-yellow grain of benches
polished smooth by generation upon generation of backsides.
What stayed mundane was the sermon,
big words children had no need to understand
to enter the heaven of the sun.
How lonnnnggg-winded he was, Gawddd,
boring, boring, boring rote out of the preacher's mouth
till you wanted him to swallow a fly -
I pinched my arm to keep awake.

But when the choir rose in their white blouses,
their singing whelmed through my lungs
like light though the tall stained windows,
I followed not the verses of the hymn
but the hum of our voices as they flowed
out the oaken doors, over the rolling hills,
down the hollow and flashed across the creek
as dozens of dragonfly wings.

After the service, the women in their floral
polyester dresses, gossiped in knots
and old men uncomfortably in starched collars
gathered around beat-up pick-up trucks
splattered with the same red clay they came from,
spit long strings of tobacco juice and talked low
down in a way I leaned toward.

I edged away from the candied condescensions
of the preacher and found my body released
to the field suddenly golden, all hallelujah
breaking loose as I ran and ran,
and stood whirling still--circled by trees full
of cicadas rasping their seventeen year prayer
stoked by gusts of solar flares
that blessed also my face.

Falling to earth then, I laid there below
the head-tall hay a long while listening
to the dull cartilage of grasshoppers clattering
aloft from stem to stem, to the dipsy doodle songs
that startled a mockingbird's throat as if
for the first time, to the green river unravelling
through the shade-maples, their fat leaves
upturned hosannas and closer, to the crickets
burrowed under the dark soil, scraping the husks
of their bodies into music--all the callings
that I followed, that I follow now
into the other world from which this world grows
into singing light.

> *Though we've been here*
> *10,000 years,*
> *bright shining as the sun,*
> *we've no less days*
> *to sing God's praise*
> *then when we first begun.*

The Sustenance of Light

Every winter grey skies for Mass for Sundays on end.
Inside dim, immigrant cathedral, arches holding space open
glowed with Medieval weight. I stared up and up.
Huge on the ceiling over the altar's
gleaming bazaar, over the cassocked priest
gesturing us to rise as a body,
over the crucifix, the light of the world
contorted there,
over it all on outstretched wings, the holy ghost
sailed hosanna on the highest.

Light, I saw, could blaze golden, carrying me away
from Cleveland where it can sleet or snow or both
for more than forty days easy, clouds sliding
low and steady off Lake Erie in layers as continuous
as the shale that hardened beneath the inland sea
that once covered these parts and receded long before
the Holy Roman Empire
raised its pinnacles.
And long time before palls of smoke sagged
down from stacks of plants in the Flats,
where haggard faced steelmen shuffled off nightshifts
through gates of mills into dawn rain of iron filings.

All during the service, I watched pale seraphims
pause red and blue in the stained glass,
falling mottled on the doughy faces of the faithfull.
On both sides of the altar, row upon row,
the hearts of the departed
flickered present -- Grandfather among them,
singing off a week's drudgery with the choir.
When the chalky effluvium wafted from the censer
and tingled my nose, I believed I smelled the burning bones
of ancient Saints ascending. The bells shivered
when the host was held aloft, small as a solstice sun.
It was what we had come for and it was broken
and passed down the line onto anemic tongues,
dissolving in the smouldering murk of each body.

After Mass, huddles of babushkas, their English
knocked loose from clumps of old country earth
like "bahdayduhs" as Grandma called them,
their breaths steaming dumpling soup,
plowed through the swirls of snow-flurries and fly-ash
from the Illuminating Company.
As they hurried home, pigeons scattered from the sidewalk,
hopping and flapping up
above the cross--the cross silhouetted
against the smudge of December sun.

Winter Holy Water

Old skin shivering,
young skin shivering,
hardly bundled mourners
somber forward in the snowfall
that whispers into the grave.

Clustered together, voices
ghost the air reciting
assurances, teeth chattering
between responses.

Wanting to blow
into bare hands,
clap arms
around bodies,
stamp the ground,
all suffer
the same weather.

Young fingers tingle
as if touching metal.
They clutch cards with Jesus' heart
on one side, and black letters
tracked across the other.

His face clotted, the grey priest
leads the last prayers
numb mouths huff and fumble.
He shakes holy water
on the casket that freezes
instantly as breath.

Old Woman in a Slovenian Church in Cleveland

Her husband gone years ago yet her requiem
hums through diffuse light conducive to mourning.
Her tongue flickers like a red-cupped candle.

She keeps arthritic hands warm with the flow
of solid beads, the seeds of the departed
she plants over and over, rising as black wheat.

She tells her decades every evening during novenas,
creaking Hail Marys in an accent that trickles
down the gutters of a village in Slovenia.

Her devotions hover and ascend as she ceases,
roosting in darkness as deep as her upturned eyes.

The Purgatory of Sister Margaret Merciless

Back in the days when a nun was a nun,
black swathed and Inquisitional,
Excalibur crucifix swinging from her waist,
Sister Margaret Merciless proved purgatory existed
no matter what Vatican II said.
Every afternoon at Immaculate Misconception

we suffered numbers, rigid as right angles in our desks.
I winced when she called me to the board
with a brogue as thick and inflexible
as the yardstick always at her side,
"Number 6, Raymond!" Inevitably the one
story problem I could not figure all homework long.

Shuffling clumsy and doomed
through the Cartesian co-ordinates of the desks,
the blackboard looming like the walls of perdition,
I knew I had but 3 minutes to luck up
the one, holy, correct and absolute answer.
"If Bobby digs a ditch 6' deep
by 6' long, and extends a plank
at a 75 degree angle to the bottom, what would be
St. Augustine's doctrines on the venal sins -- squared!"
I kept digging, the chalk blunting
to a pill, my lungs filling
with the pure dust of mathematics.

Fixed between the stern and set vertices
of her face, her habit an even darker wall closing in,
she scrutinized my fallibility.
"No, that's not it. Try again."
I turned back to the rickety gallows I was deconstructing,
hand cramping as I smeared away lame guesses, chalk thick
on blue uniform and clip-on tie,
burning like quicklime when I rubbed tear blurred eyes.

Classmate after classmate redeemed themselves
and resumed sitting, leaving me to my separate penance.
How much easier it would have been to scrawl
"I will not put fishfood on Sister Margaret's sandwich,"
one hundred and fifty times after school.
I pictured her next to St. Peter at the Gate,
an enormous eraser in one hand, in the other
the ruler she measured our knuckles with so quickly.

Stalling, I tried to block the numbers
that would not even stay in line
let alone arrive at an answer,
with the single digit of my shrinking body.
"Well, Raymond, have you finished yet?"
as if I were at the urinal in the Boys room.
Flush-faced, I turned, guilty of ignorance,
sloth, and probably some other unmentionable sin.
"Wrong again." And again I was consigned
to the limbo of the D student.

She called on the class genius then.
He clicked forward, blinking binary,
a computer before there were chips,
and solved it in a cinch.
In him I saw the future, infinitely numerical,
where I could not count.
All summer vacation I nightmared the problem,
the floor opening before I could get it right,
my nails scrapping the blackboard
like a cat out of lives,
her cackle taunting me as I plummeted,
"I told you to do your homework!"
The condemnation I hear when I land
among the tormented figures of my tax return
limping to get in under the April 15th deadline.

From the Shining Eyes Staring Back From the Woods

We left behind the brightly-lit night life of the city
closing in on us lonely and womanless
for this mountain rising above Penobscot Bay.
Gathering together whatever deadfall we could
find in the dusk, we start a fire orange as origins.
Winter gusts rush clattering through the last
yellow poplar leaves and swirl sparks
upward into the stars, which, by considering
ground us in the smouldering murk of our bodies.
We drink dark beer confiding the sweet mysteries
and joys bones can know before the dream of flesh
and blood wears away and we become kindling again.

You bring up "The World, The Flesh, The Devil"
we had to renounce in our nun-instructed,
guilt-controlled days of parochial school.
Mass was one, glorious, elaborate tease --
candles, incense, wine and the tongue outstretched --
then we were married eternally to the church.
The constancy of the white surplice replaced
any ecstasy of skin. Suddenly we were choirboys
dogmatized to venerate a virgin on a pedestal,
sneaking a peak up her robe if we could.
The sullen, mitered bishop hanging between our legs,
who we were never allow to touch let alone
play with, rose in spite when we flogged him
for his dirty thoughts -- rose as stern as Paul's
exhortation that the Church should always be
"the pillar of God against the gates of Hell."

I scratch a figure in the dirt by the fire,
an outline of the antlerman drawn by a shaman
deep in a cave 20,000 years ago. He turns,
poised to dance, his pronounced cock ready
to enact the ritual vitalities of hunch and strut,
of tup and rut with his consort, the bulbous
Our Lady of Mud, their coupling unabashed.
Once, as children, we ran naked on the shore,
dived into the surf, jigging up and down the waves,
sun-brown arms upraised, peckers hard in the cold.
We played ourselves out until we simply dropped
into that good tired only the body can know.
After hiking all day, we feel it again, watching
wind stoke the fire that glows with the same
energy of genesis that comes from the core of us,
from the shining eyes staring back from the woods.

Annunciation

How could the almond trees
outside her window resist
the spring and not burst
into humming pungency?
How could she resist
the naive light of his face
or how his body
gently spread its wings?
He was so young, and she was
married to an old, kind
provider, sturdy as the tables
he made that she would set
with the fruits of the earth.
But she grew empty
washing away the moon
gone bloody every month.
How could he resist the sway
of her body as she ground grain.
Suddenly tired of searching,
he felt the root of his groin
push towards the earth.
Never had a woman's hands
held him with such strength.
Never had the terrifying
weight of life rested on him.
After, without asking his name,
she sent him on his way.
The elders told of how
Joseph's branch sprouted anew,
but the washerwomen knew.
They saw the stranger leave,
his face glowing with sorrow.

Baptism

For weeks afterwards
you kept waking, asking
your father for water.
Once you kept the light on
and the lampshade off,
but it threw the shadows
larger,. gnarled like claws
ready to drag you down
to hell and once there,
as the preacher had said,
you would not get a drop
if you were not saved.

He picked out you alone
among the chosen lined up.
"You, young lady, right there!
You could die tomorrow
and because you have not
accepted Lord as salvation,
you would be cast down
and wedged in a hole
where you could plead and weep,
and gnash your teeth,
where no matter how dry
you got, you would not
get one solitary drop."

You remember the hot breath
of the town filling the tent,
and how the preacher's eyes
bulged and his slicked hair
dripped sweat as he hurled
aside the microphone
and rushed towards you--
this same man who smacked
mutes on the forehead shouting,
"Out you devil! Out!"
The only time you witnessed
a smack like that was when
you father, home late drunk,
answered your mother
slap for slap for slap.

The entire assembly did not
take their eyes off you.
Their stares were stones
ready to cast at a sinner.
Now you would be found
out, no denying, no escape
from God or this man
who smelled of mouthwash
and something sulphurous
when he embraced you
in his polyester suit.

When you were finally
doused, your head forced
under and bathed in the blood
of our saviour, you stood there,
hair matted back, shivering,
and cried. And he told you
"Now look at your parents,
so proud." When you turned
you could not tell them
from the disembodied faces.

Afterwards, you never felt
sweet love flowing through you.
No matter how much water
you drank before falling to sleep,
you woke parched and afraid
to ask your father for more.
You nightmared God admonishing
down with a bony finger,
then holding an eyedropper.
Below him, hairless and blind,
your thin neck straining,
you clapped your mouth on nothing.

The Stretch of River Between Belpre and Marietta

Never since the chemical plants
and refineries raised their shining bodies
to begin seething, shift after shift,
has the river in these stretches
my father told of
spoken its own name.

Oh, it wanted to, many summers
as it limped by doomed elms that pulled it up
and spread it leaf-taut.
Along some sloughs corn still stands still,
sheening and June-full.

At the confluence with the Muskingum,
there are men with farmer's tans--
the kind where your throat, biceps and neck
are burning, and the rest of your skin is untouched--
there are men wading and fishing with doughballs
for the channel cats that plow down
and down, eating, cleaning,
remembering the current's curves.

On their way to work at the plant,
they don't have time to lament much
of what passes.
My cousin who has worked there for years
gets nosebleeds sometimes for no reason.
For no real reason, the preacher says,
the kids around here
are blowing their minds out.

When the river bends around
around by Belpre,
even under the cover of darkness,
it will not utter a single vowel or ripple
of its origins and changes
because there it is--
cylindrical, illuminated, steaming, manifested--
the plant stands and hums.
And the river there moves like a rat snake
through a sewer pipe.

On a day the sun was doing everything it could
to make the water appear half-healthy,
on a bluff above Marietta, the sulphur upwind,
we watched as you spoke for yourself, for us,
for all the good it would do,
you said, Ohio, and again,
muddling along, Ohio.

Skinnydipping the Ganges

Too many times I simply cannot think
without thinking. Biceps and thighs break
free of this as I dive and stroke
up through the cold spring, sunfilled pond,
the pale flame of my body
burning underwater.

Then, there they are, sides glinting --
a dim arc curling,
a cluster of sharp flashes scattering --
and I see how thoughts come to light
then angle back
into the green blending to black deeps
and again rise

where ice-melt sings flashes
clear down from the Himalyas
in the thrum of minnows
the current carries to the plain of the Ganges
where a young woman,
so used to the task,
balances a plaited basket full of silver slivers
on her head
as she scuffs along the dust

thinking of nothing,
humming to herself
beside a river that is always finding
easy ways -- swallowing villages,
birthing fields --
while the sun is on fire
the whole time
as a thought itself.

Waking At Evening

I slept all afternoon
to stay out of the heat.
Now towards evening
my pulse takes the pace
of a quarter-horse
stumping its way
up a worn incline
in its own good plod
to a blue-green pasture.

He basks in the dusk
and munches remnants
of oats from his gums
into a sweet paste,
and dumps warm briquets.

His coat ripples loose.
His flanks relax.
His belly, having pulled
a long drink, hangs
as content as after
the rutting season.

He swishes, then rubs,
then leans against
a split-rail fence
rottening with moss.

Summers ago I watched
this horse standing up
asleep and wondered
at such heavy ease.
This evening, walking
alongside his bulk,
I sway into waking.

Winter Solstice

Late December grinds on down.
The sky stops, slate on slate,
scattering a cold light of snow
across a field of brittle weeds.

Each bootstep cracks a stalk.
The pigments have been dragged
earthwards and clasped. The groundhog
curls among the roots curling.

Towards home I peel blossoms
of frozen mud from my pant legs
and pull off burrs that waited
for wind or the flashing red fox.

In my jacket pocket I find
a beechnut, slightly open,
that somehow has fallen there.
And, enfolded inside of it,

a spider that unclenches
yellow in my steaming palm --
a spider that is the sun.

Dogwood Blossoms

Chest tightened, oppressed
by too much busyness,
I've come to this creek
right beside the rapids,
to drop my heart in.

It bounces off the worn
rocks, off the sand bottom,
scuffing up bits of algae
and swirling black mulch.

Minnows nip at the fat
hangings-on and the clots.
They enter aortas,
jiggle around inside
the four relaxed fists
and dart out again.

On the day I gave up
fishing as an easy way
to relax, I hooked a chub
deep in its shriveled
gullet with three prongs.

Twisting in my numb hand,
it squealed, gills flapping
blood, and I kept pulling
and pulling.

           All winter
I've strained and stayed
caught in senseless routines,
felt anger clench and beat
to a dull ache. But the bruises
in my chest open into broad
dogwood blossoms here
and float and slip into
and into and into...

After Talking Long Into The Night

Walking out, nearly out of my mind
meddling around the strange arrangement
of stars and space, the time continuum --
those final questions of our conversation --
unable to stop thinking up and up,
I give in to the cricket's dull chirrup

Coming From Fathoms Down Where Impulses Glow

Coming from fathoms down where impulses glow
like lantern-fish basking along molted edges
of cracks that stem from the core;

coming around the bend of light years where stars
kindle, whiz and pinwheel like pinefire sparks
brightening the dark before snuffing out;

coming back from torchlit caves where fingers trace
charcoal and ocher outlines of animals on walls,
giving solid shape and proof to dreamtime charms;

coming from the translucent pulse of amoebas,
coming from the blinding heart of supernovas,
I've arrived again, ready, willing and able to face

this hard miracle of another turn around the sun,
saying I am and blowing it all away the same day
with a last breath birthday candle wish of light.

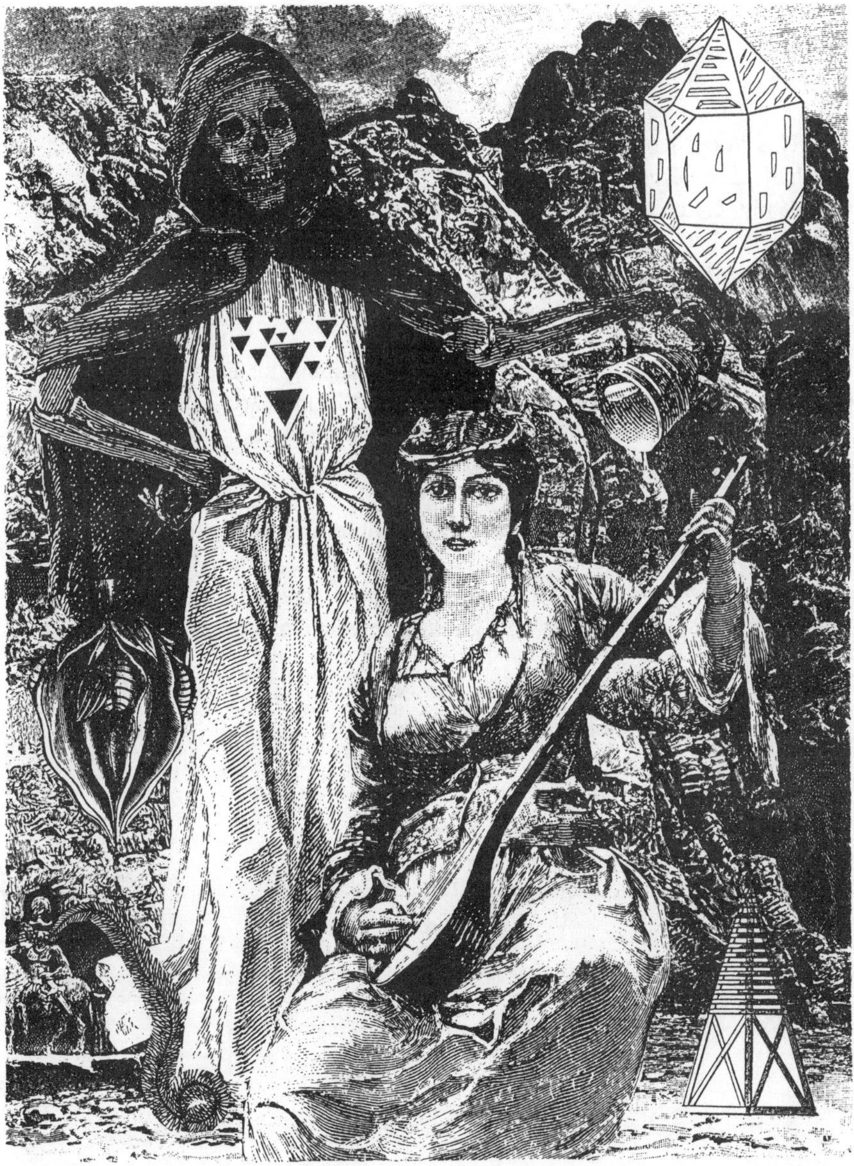

Once You Uncover

Once you uncover your several insane ancestors,
do you think it is ever possible to bury them all again?
They stand in those insomnia hallways and stare,
each, in turn, pointing at you wearing thin your skin.

This body is one crowded European sanitarium --
half-saints dressed in shivers, would-be Slavic kings,
gaudy, calico fools. Others that are only vague whims.
Mongrel hybrids, rut-smelling, tearing at their rags.
A girl who would collapse into flame at a touch.
Some collide, shudder -- scar-tissue eyes, cave fish.

There's an Irish monk, bald from god slapping his head,
jarred loose from his love of Jesus and Virgin Mary,
who lifted his sack-cloth, whose goat thighs pulsed
and begot fanatical lovers of gods and bodies.

And I hear that Slovenian woman mumble as she unwinds
the fringe of her robe -- strands of gold, saliva, root-hair --
then sews a new gown, tense as skin, these scraps I wear,
the crazy stitched seams and knotted threads inside.

Snapshots of the Void

I split. Spliiiiiiit --
went where you go when you
go a little toooooooo far and almost
didn't make it back
together. Panicked up,
lungs flapping, sight flashing
black and bright, being
being sucked down,
lightning
splintering.

Sat shocked inside
bare, white room,
undernerve endings
fibrillating
through bare bulb.
I could see like no
eyelids, no matter how
I tried not to
stare into insomnia's
nightmirror, mouthing nothing
that would get me...out.

So, no, I'm not just a tourist
of the abyss anymore,
gawking in, waving, posing
for Polaroid snapshots
like a yokel from Ohio --
bzzzp...bzzzp...bzzzp--
neat squares of the void
to show the folks back home.

No, last night my little
propeller beanie got blown
over the edge and I
clutched after it.
See, here's one of me
panicking up.

The White Birds of Purgatory

After her shower she feels more sane.
The smell of disinfectant on her skin
and the change of pajamas calm her.
She pinches her cheeks for color.
There, clean and ready for visitors.
"I will give up the binge and purge."
"I will give up the binge and purge."

In the visiting room waiting,
she can't stop glancing at Van Gogh's
cut flowers, staggered and turgid,
the yellows stuck on the greens,
the color of half-digested food.
She pictures his bandaged head.
She jammed a spoon down her throat.

A patient's still-life of basin
and pitcher tilts on the far wall --
cool, blue porcelin, a design
she'd like to trace fingers over
if only she could touch what it is.
She runs her tongue over teeth
scorched chalky by stomach acid.

Her face reflected in the unbreakable
plastic of the exit-door window hangs
drugged, as long as an El Greco Saint's.
She stays neither here nor there.
No burning. No singing. Only thorazine
and linen. She's made up her mind
to leave for good this time if they let her.

"Every meal this huge girl flops down
across from me. I'm the only one
who talks to her. She carved I HATE MYSELF
across both her wrists twice. If I
kept stuffing myself I'd look in the mirror
just like her in a year. I had to stop here
or end up on a slab in the morgue."

"But I'm getting it under control.
The smell of the sheets helps
when I can't sleep or when I get real
hungry I lay face down and inhale for hours.
But some nights I just want to run and
run all the way to Indiana and crawl
into a clapboard church and sleep inside God.

I keep painting. And writing too.
Letters to my mother trying to forgive
her for calling me FAT, FAT, FAT! and
hiding cakes for herself. They need
to unlock the elevators to let you down.
Don't worry, last night I dreamed white birds
flew out of my body and returned at dawn.
They settled flat and clean on my desk."

Before the Downturn of the Bloodwheel

She listens into the dark, and her pulse,
a dull viola bowing over and over,
pulls as the music she must release.

But she cannnot bring herself to dance
the urge that in so many turns, says,
you are only gathered in this shape once.

She knows the rite of blood is that is rises,
that it arrives, fully her, from each cell --
that love would loosen the drag of her menses.

So she lifts up and shuffles the narrow
hallway out of her rooms, out of the burden
of the swollen moon, almost glissando

out along the river she always hears,
and her shadow, a few free steps ahead,
wavers blue-black and thinning on the water.

She slides asleep there next to the slow
tugging and dreams of wings pushing through.
Heaving as she would, she watches a crow

mate with a crow. They thrive as one
vulnerable body, half-flying, half-falling
their praise to weight and lightness of blood.

Young Woman Crossing a Field

The grown-over field along the freeway
stands mostly as real-estate, a square lot
of useless scrub at a practical glance.
A good location for condos or a shopping center.
She takes her time to picture corn rising.

One long stare and her everyday eyes
no longer overlook the sight -- the field
contours to its former symmetries:
dark smelling furrows open, and stalks line,
chlorophyl-vibrant, to yellow flaring heights.

But the traffic keeps up its droning.
Shafts of sunlight splinter through the cloud plates
and sweep across the brush. The wind embers colors.
Here and there creatures are hidden, dying
or alive from the inside out, a caterpillar's body.

She lies down below the weedtops,
but hears her mother complaining again,
"Really, you never see things as they are."
Stick-tights and burrs snag the blouse
She was never supposed to get dirty.

She pulls handfulls, studies their shapes,
and sows them. Turning, she looks at the field
again and feels it fluxing through her older
and younger. A quail bobs through the undergrowth
somewhere out of sight, its berryblack eyes glistening.

Hide and Seek

All last night's worried
turning, I ended up
ghosting along moon-shown
Forest Hills cemetery roads
where I met this kid
climbing a marble mausoleum.
You live here? we asked
each other. No, we echoed,
tombstone smiles mirroring.

Awake, I breathe backwards,
playing hide and seek,
the kid scrunched inside
skull and crossbones ready
to spring out. He taught me to
tip-toe tap dance grave lips,
how to throw voices through
doorways into the dark easy
as a hoot owl screeching down
between bare limbs to strike
the corpse rat to the quick --

"Quick, over here." His hands
toads, jumping into a tomb
still as moss. "Quick now, here."
his hands flaring shadowy
inscriptions of stone poems
eaten away by wind and rain...
"Unless spoken out loud," says
a plume of breath becoming
a face pretending to be
a played out, layed out wisp
whispering, "Closer, come closer."
His moon face wavers in a well,
his hand palsies a beckoning:
"Closer, come -- Tag! You're it."

Disneyland

There's a thin line...between in and sane...
one nerve...pin it down here...
pin it down over here...see what I mean...
don't push me into a corner on this one...there's four
walls here...I'm inside of 'em...
reality?...who's kidding who?
reality...sillyputty...
press it to the headlines...the pictures of the catastrophic dead...
press it...twist it...
what a show...what really happened:
don't pop a vein in your head worryin' about it...
what's eatin' me alive...is makin' a livin'...
I live with it...all I have to do
for my two weeks vacation
all I have to do...is go back
and forth...one of these days
I'm gonna go and I'm gonna keep on goin' forever...
I'm gonna walk through walls...
I'm gonna walk through time...
I'm gonna shed my skin and go the speed of light...
one of these days...
whatever you do...whatever you do...
don't go to the zoo...saddest part about the panther...
it's the paw...the way it goes
flop...flop...
flop...don't look in their eyes...
there's nowhere to go...I've been around...
where you won't be in the middle of a shopping mall...
did I have a hand in it? Ask the extinct...
the dinosaurs...for instance...
we ate their eggs...us...
we climbed outa the trees at night with our beady little eyes...
our grubby little hands...
our sharp little teeth...we sucked 'em dry...
we were quick...had to be...
we went right back up those trees...
right back up those trees...
I still like eggs...scrambled...

over-easy...sunny-side-up...
Disneyland...oh boy...remember?
you stand in line for hours...
to watch machines having fun...
you're in a tour boat...in a fake lagoon...
you're in a tour boat floating along
all the sudden...boom!
fake explosion...wheeeeeeeeee
fake whistling...Whoosh!
fake geyser of water...
then the herky-jerky
swashbuckling of Captain Hook
and his mechanical laughter...Ha-ha-ha!...
even Peter Pan is goin' through the motions
even Peter Pan...but everyone laughs and claps anyway...
the tour boat floats along...
watch out for the fake crocodile...
you're just about to round a bend...
boom! wheeeeeeeeee...whoosh!
everyday...for years on end...
my mother got stuck on a ride...it's a small world after all...
it's a small world...through the years
we'll all be there...there's a blue child
thumpin' his wings against the tube...
see what I mean...one nerve...
it's not an electrical cord...can't be plugged in...
whatever you do...don't go to the zoo...
it's a POW camp...don't look in their eyes...
nope...don't look in their eyes...

CRAZY HEART
      (for Sergio Mayora)

Hey, Crazy! Loco, Coyote. Ho Ka Hay! It's me,
Buddy. Broke, broken-winged, busted heart-string Buddy.
Don't be shovellin' dirt on my face yet,
I gotta nasty habit of pullin' a Finnegan's wake on ya.
Remember? I was last seen doin' that age-old do-ci-do
with my shadow, followin' those Fred Astaire cut-out foot prints
doubled up across the dance floor lookin' like Fred Flintstone
empty pockets hangin' out, pants 'bout ready to drop down
'round by ankles, the shoestring budget seriously frayed...
but still keepin' the beat to memory's marimba
that delicate rhythmic hemorrhaging -- El Corazon Sangriente...
Spinnin' this way like every woman who ever walked out on me,
spinnin' that way like every woman I ever walked out on,
straight out that revolving door.

I was out there at the intersection of Desperation Drive
and Oblivion Boulevard for hours,
scouring the gutter for that lost number for the last call,
love letter obituaries blowin' between my legs,
clutchin' a one-way ticket down a dead-end street,
trying' to hitch a ride to a sunset Hollywood ending --
or at least a bus to Cleveland.
I knew I had just enough umpf left for maybe
one final fandango, on last leap of faith
to the end of my rope -- a hangman's knot -- I fell flat
on my aspirations. (It's not the falling, it's the landing.)
A cat, Crazy, may have nine lives, but a dog --
a dog ain't got but one, this raggedy tail
I chased all night doin' the down the drain drag
till the cows came home to roost.

Crazy, remember? I was holdin' up that end of the bar
with the other members of the busted balls club,
comparin' our open-heart surgery scars, showin' off
our blue I-love-you tatoos blurrin' into the fat of our biceps,
tryin' to find yet another title and plot line for the same
old done-me-wrong-song that drones on and on
till somebuddy in the back booth shouts shut-up already about her!
before he slumps asleep, her drowned name surfacing
one last time on his bloated sailor lips
so it sounded like her name like a wave of the sea...
empty...empty as the fifteenth shot of tequila
might as well embalm my heart and send it to the Louvre.
Let a French art student swallow it whole.
She Frankensteined me! Took me apart limbo by limbo
and put me back together with all the other stiffs
who couldn't quite fit her little fine-print list--
I felt like a crash-test dummy by the end of it!

Crazy, I been down at the crossroads a long time now.
Down that way YES always sounds like always once upon a time.
Down that way NO echoes on and on through hollow towns
where the blue flame of late nite movies
licks the ceilings of upstairs bedrooms.
Back there, Cleveland. I ain't goin' back to Cleveland yet.
I know I ain't got no choice but to live with my choices.
And I know even escape from desire is desire.
So which way is home when there's nothin' there
but an empty bed, an empty name pulled out
from the deepest wound of night, echoing the moon-bare room.

Once I thought home was a woman.
Once I thought home was a poem about a woman.
And once I found home in my worn-down shoes
doin' the prayer of the feet that carried me out
to that intersection. Crazy, remember, I was the one
standin' on the berm among the other road kills
that never saw what hit 'em. I was holdin' up
that cardboard sign said HOME on it -- you picked me up.
You told me, "Home, Bro, is the heart --
where all the roads lead, where all the roads start."
Crazy, remember?

First Woman on The Moon

This song is gravity
pulling the dead light
from the full moon
into the lungs and sung
from the top of the escape
alone and above love
filling the empty alley.

She's up there alright,
bounding dunes weightlessly,
somersaulting crators,
deserted evening gown
fluttering through the dark
like breath through an oboe.
And she's not coming back.

Who hears the sad chant
of the crickets at dawn?
Who hears the whippoorwill
anymore? Hank, stop drinking
that milk laced with whiskey
and tell me, who hears
the moon going down solo?

Night Song

You lovers who lie alone from each other
in the same dark and listen, listen to this:

when the cricket screams into the calcium moon
that pulls both of your bodies and fuses there

so that full through the night it will be pain
quickened so close to you, you might hear

how whatever anxious magic persists and quivers
that cartilage husk into music, tightens me.

But how can I tell that you feel how the skeleton
becomes the teeth that close around one, how the spine,

serrated, becomes the tense spur, or how frantically
the cricket scrapes away inside the bone-insane moon?

What for the sake of love can I hopefully say to you
of how a woman tried to separate the splintered words

from this flesh to free the body's song from intellect
with her flush hands, her momentary mouth and tongue,

when all the while, all I could hear or feel, here
inside, was the crickets body raking across itself?

Then listen, when the moon and pain gave up, she began
to ease into the song we each know by now by heart.

The Skin of Oroboros

I used to love to dive
into pure sleep, feet
and pale hands digging
under the warm mud
near the evening bank,
the Chagrin River taking
and giving my body back.

The last thing I saw
last night under the black
and blue sky before
I forced my self to sleep
like a pill down my throat,
the last thing I saw
was this world now
set down in newsprint
that stained my fingertips
that smudged on your thigh.

I never have loved using
another's body as a blanket
to cover my own shiverings.
What we shared was fear,
what I wanted was a river
to carry us from our nerves
to ease.

I knew that woman.
Her skin in the secret places
she revealed was scar tissue
so taut I could not
touch her without a blossom
of pain starting. She had been
seared in her first marriage.
The second time through hell,
her shrink stood as a father
to her. She trusted his hands.
We clutched body against body,
pressed bruises in the dark,
our sharp kisses like sutures.

Last night the fear I travelled
became a city so full of teeth
that every body fell torn apart --
women, the old and the soft,
their mouths, their groins;
children splintered into
chicken bones, a greasy smear
on the sidewalk; and grown men
withered out on yellowing cots
in warehouses of uselessness
like dry, brown roots
gone to stone and broken.

Before that night-mirror could
scab over, I pulled awake,
lungs drowning with breathings
and sweated across the sheets.
Holding you, letting go with you,
I remembered Oroboros, the circling
snake sloughing off its wasted flesh,
swallowing end as beginning --
the river that closes fresh
and cool over our bodies.

The Inevitable Movement of Love

Mothers warned their daughters of sailors,
but who warned the sailors of you
and all your candles. As you touch your fire
to the last wicks that forest and cathedral the dark,
you tell me what the Swedish wive's tale tells --
"everytime you light a candle, you kill a sailor."

Many sailors have died in this bedroom
where you lead me to dance unsteady
on my sea-legs of champagne, giddy
with your praise of how I always move
towards what I love as I move now
towards your flushed and flickering body.

Our coming together is the inevitable movement of love,
two lives fastening before groaningly letting go,
invoking god to come, come and show us your face,
our eyes rolling back into our skulls,
obliterating mathematics with the equation
one plus one equals one, intimate wisdom
that widens out into the phosphorescence of stars
where we sink and sleep like luminous fish.

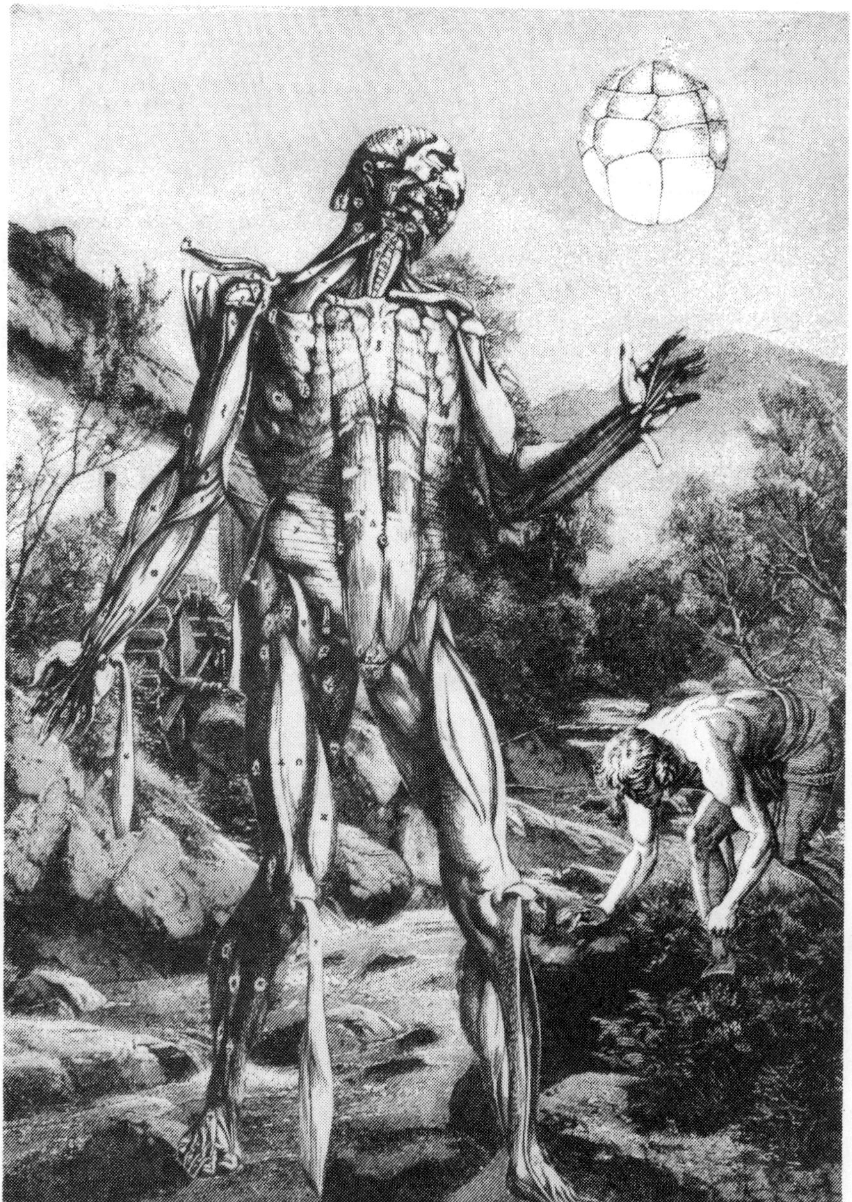

Fly
to the Nuyorican Poet's Cafe

I don't know if I wanna go back up there.
Oh you can see so far when you're that high
and all I ever wanted was to fly,
flapping away my boyhood along the cliff edges,
gathering feathers together to make a cape
to spread as golden as the sun -- to kiss that fire.
Dazzled. Buzzin' all day. Frazzled by nightfall
so there was nowhere to land in that big drink
where I would not sizzle and sink like shark-bait.

Yet another crash and burn lesson to be learned
face to face with my own ignorance.
You think hell has only one floor?
I nose-dived straight to the bargain basement,
groped around the dank piles of empty egos
to find my barely beating heart, a faint glow
I blew on to warm my hands till it smoldered up
illuminating obscenities scrawled on walls
by broken fingers. I blew nooo! and it all curled open again --

that drunken passion soap-opera, a cartoon Don Juan
done by a yokel from Ohio, New York debut screw-up.
I tried daring arias, falsetto falling apart like a cheap
suit, and they clapped and clapped as the trap
door opened and the devils of every failure
pulled my shot-a-whiskey spirit down the drain
to the strains of toy violins and the drum roll
of my bones, rimshots shattering my brain-pan
leaving behind nothing but a clot of skin and hair
at my feet and this standing autopsy of a poseur
like day-old fried chicken shrivelling under a hot lamp.

I bragged how I'd sing, believed I had wings --
my hands suddenly pulled up by strings
that wouldn't let me fend off the wads of laughter.
So I did a lewd jig to dodge the catcalls,
but they only howled more and gravity
got ahold of me then, down for the count.
But it wasn't over yet. Not till I vomited every cliche.
But even that wasn't the finale. I still had to spit out
that maggot at the root of vanity, how fat it's gotten,
gorged on such a portion of pride, such a mess of lies.
And I did finally spit it out, squirming for all to see.
But even maggots know the secrets of wings.

So I step back into these shoes full of ashes,
pluck the chintzy gold sequins from this charred flesh,
and kick up my heels. I'll show you how I leap
with only this thin line delicately attached to the edge,
these strands I weave so I can hang out suspended,
eyes in every direction, a belly full of fire, and such a kiss.
But you know as well as I do that there is no
net...not even...a...tightrope..and we like it up here.